Low-cost Vehicles

Low-cost Vehicles

Options for moving people and goods

GORDON HATHWAY

INTERMEDIATE TECHNOLOGY PUBLICATIONS 1985

Intermediate Technology Publications,
9 King Street, London WC2E 8HW.

ISBN 0 946688 40 0 (Hardback)
      0 946688 02 8 (Paperback)

Printed in Great Britain by Photobooks Ltd, Bristol

CONTENTS

Acknowledgements

The authors wish to thank the following for pictures used: J. Collett for those on pages 34, 57, 60, 66, Earthscan for page 25, the FAO for page 18, Terry Fincher of Photographers International for page 90, Elizabeth Hoddy for page 23, Dr Seoul Kim for pages 26, 27, 39, 41, 61, 62, 75, 103, the WHO for pages 17, 19, 44, and the UNA for pages 22, 23, 31.

All other photographs came from the archives of Intermediate Technology Transport.

PART ONE

Transport means the movement of people and goods ...

THE PROCESS and means of moving people and goods are normally referred to as 'transport', whether the means involved is a bicycle or an oil tanker. In the industrialized nations the term has become synonymous with motor cars, trucks, buses, trains, ships and aircraft, because those are the means of transport most commonly used there. In developing countries these methods of transport are also used, but they are much less important to the majority of people. Most people do not have access to vehicles of this sort, which therefore cannot meet many of their needs.
More important to the poor are forms of local land transport, based on the use of simple vehicles which are inexpensive to own and operate, and which can travel over the narrow paths and unmade roads which form the largest part of the route network they have to use. It is this kind of transport which is the concern of this book.

... but it is more than just large vehicles on major routes.

Transport authorities, whether governmental or independent, are rarely concerned with any type of transport other than large vehicles on major routes. Organizations with other primary concerns, such as agriculture or health, often address themselves to problems of 'access', 'availability', 'distribution' and 'mobility', but they do not usually refer to a specific need for transport. The purpose of this book is to highlight the fact that transport is necessary in many different fields of activity, and to show that there are many more ways of meeting transport needs than just by using large vehicles on major routes.

Transport is needed for many reasons ...

Transport is different from other 'needs', such as the need for food or housing, in that it is required only to *enable* other activities to take place. It enables people to obtain access to services, or to work away from their home, or to make visits; it enables goods to be marketed; it enables materials to be gathered, and used where they are wanted. The total transport requirements of a society encompass many permutations of different types of load, of different sizes and weight, to be moved over different distances and types of terrain. It is worth giving some general examples in various fields of activity in order to identify the types of transport need with which this book is concerned.

... in agriculture ...

In developing countries most

1

agricultural work is carried out on small farms to produce subsistence crops and, where possible, surpluses to create cash income. It can be argued, as the FAO has done, that the farmer is, above all, a transporter. Tools, fertilizer, seeds and produce must all be moved between field, store and market, and transporting them is often the single most time-consuming activity. The means of transport used therefore has a very important effect on overall productivity, and it may play a crucial role in determining whether surplus crops can be marketed successfully.

... in business ...

All businesses involve communication, by telephone, by letter and also by personal visits to customers, suppliers and other contacts. In places where other forms of communication are poor, personal travel is particularly important in conducting business. Manufacturing and trading companies rely on transport for the delivery of materials and goods, and for the distribution of finished products to customers. The cost and efficiency of the means of transport employed can have a significant effect on profitability and success.

... in domestic work ...

Two tasks which dominate domestic work for many people are the collection and movement of fuel and water. The method of transport most commonly used is simply to carry loads on the head, shoulder or back. Frequently it is women who do these tasks, and it is unusual for any

kind of equipment or vehicle to be used which would reduce the amount of time or effort involved. Domestic work may also involve travelling to a town or market to purchase food or other goods. The frequency of such trips and the places visited are conditioned by the type and cost of the transport which is available.

... in education ...

Education is largely concerned with providing people with access to information and learning facilities. Whether those resources are taken to where people live, or whether people travel to a central school or college, a need for transport still exists. In rural areas the level of access to a school, and the means of transport available, can have a crucial influence on the effectiveness of the educational service — on the supply of teaching materials, on the provision of management and support services and on the willingness of teachers to work at a particular place. Equally these factors will influence the attendance at the school.

... in health care ...

Health care is similarly concerned with providing people with access to medical facilities and personnel. The problems of providing access are often acute. It is difficult for people who are ill to travel very far, particularly if walking is the only means of transport available. With the trend towards decentralization of facilities, and greater use of paramedical staff to visit patients in their home or village, the importance of transport in providing health care increases. Equipment, medicines and other supplies have to be distributed without deterioration en route, and staff must be able to travel, often to remote locations, to reach their patients.

... and for social activities.

People in societies at every level of development attach great importance to personal mobility. The ability to travel freely, not just for practical purposes but to visit friends and relatives, or for recreation, may not be a 'basic need', but it is clearly very desirable, particularly in societies where family ties are strong. In most societies some form of personal transport, be it an animal, a bicycle or a motor car, is a prized possession. Studies of the impact of rural road programmes show that one of the most important consequences of the provision of a road is often an increase in personal travel.

Transport is essential in meeting basic needs ...

The satisfaction of 'basic needs' is a pre-eminent priority for the individual, and it is the aim of many

---

Box A   Distance and use of health facilities

• ... it was found in Kenya that 40 per cent of the outpatients attending a health centre lived within 5 miles of it, 30 per cent lived between 5 and 10 miles from it, and a further 30 per cent lived more than 10 miles away ... approximately four times as many people came from each square mile within the 0 - 5 mile zone as came from one in the 5 - 10 mile zone. The same grossly inequitable distribution of outpatient services has also been observed in Uganda.[1]

• Similar data on attendance and distance are available for a study from Lusaka[2].

Distance from hospital	Ratio of patients attending hospital
less than 5km	1 in 2
5-8km	1 in 3
9-16km	1 in 5
17-32km	1 in 17
33-40km	1 in 46

• An eye hospital serving a large area of Tanzania has recorded that 70 per cent of patients attending for the treatment of cataracts live less than 30km away. Only 20 per cent live within a radius of 30 to 50km, and just 10 per cent come from further away.

governments and aid agencies in their attempts to stimulate development. 'Basic needs' have been defined as comprising two elements:

> First, they include certain minimum requirements of a family for private consumption: adequate food, shelter and clothing, as well as certain household equipment and furniture. Second, they include essential services provided by and for the community at large, such as safe drinking water, sanitation, public transport and health, education and cultural facilities.[3]

For the individual, meeting the first element of these needs normally involves time-consuming and arduous labour in fetching water from the river or well, bringing in the harvest from the field, and gathering wood from the forest. In these terms transport is a derived need, the type and intensity of transport required being dictated by the particular needs which it is being used to satisfy.

... and improved transport is an essential part of development .

The second element of these needs is satisfied only when communities or societies can produce more than is required for subsistence alone. Since many productive activities involve moving people and goods, as the above examples show, overall productivity can often be increased by improving the means of transport employed. Where populations are widely dispersed, and resources available for providing essential services are limited, improved transport will provide better access to the services that do exist. Examples of how the accessibility of services affects the extent to which they are used are given in Box A.

Most people require local transport ...

The type of transport which people use is both that which they can afford and that which meets their immediate needs. Improved methods of transport must, of course, fulfil the same requirements. So what are these immediate needs? Relatively few surveys have examined the transport needs of the individual. Studies which have been carried out tend to focus on rural communities, and some of their important findings are presented in Box B. The results of these studies indicate that transport in rural communities has several important characteristics:

- small-scale farmers move loads of relatively small size and weight over short distances;
- subsistence-related tasks, such as cultivation and the collection of firewood and water, dominate household travel; most trips are village/community orientated; and
- many longer trips are made for social and welfare purposes.

It is reasonable to argue that, while specific trip characteristics will be different, the transport needs of poor urban communities follow a similar pattern. The majority of trips are short distance, for economic amd household purposes. Trips to and from paid work, when this is available, tend to replace those associated with agriculture.

4

Box B   Transport needs in rural areas

• A World Bank study in Kenya indicated that smallholders there generally need to move small loads (10-150kg) over relatively short distances (1-25km). For farm-based activities, loads are about the same but distances are shorter (1-13km). Domestic requirements involve moving 50kg of water and 30kg of firewood per day which takes 3-6 hours. Where additional water is required for crop spraying, 2-3 tonnes of water are required during the year to spray a half hectare of cotton — a formidable amount if headloading is used for transport.[4]

• Another report about village life in Southern and East Africa stated that in an average family of six or seven, one person's sole job is to collect firewood.[5]

• In many areas of Kenya, where family members typically find employment off the farm, passenger transport is required once or twice a month for trips back to the farm to visit the family. In general the distances involved for these trips range from 25-50km, and loads carried are small.

• A study in India revealed that 81 per cent of the weight of goods movement was within the village, with an average trip length of 1.5km. Outside the village the average trip length was 8.3km.[6]

• A study of rural mobility and communications in Mexico found that household heads travelled, on average, about 1100km. each year on journeys related to work, and over 1200km. a year for general purposes. 65 per cent of trips were local, 10 per cent regional and 25 per cent long distance.[7]

... to meet individual needs.

The best way of meeting these individual needs is to have access to a means of transport of suitable size, capability and cost. An individually-owned means of transport ensures control and availability as and when it is needed, and transport costs are not dictated by others. When transport has to be hired, most needs will be met by a service which is flexible, locally orientated and economically efficient for the carriage of small loads over short distances.

'Conventional' transport meets some needs ...

In areas where conventional motor vehicles are available they are widely used. Their availability is dependent on the existence of a system of suitable roads, and, since few people own motor vehicles, on the operation of commercial vehicles for hire on those routes. Motor vehicles are normally made available either by itinerant traders, or by private operators, co-operatives or public sector transport services. In dealing with itinerant traders the producer delegates responsibility for transporting and marketing goods by selling at the farm or factory gate. This is certainly convenient, but where no alternative means of transport exists it means that the trader can dictate terms and depress the price paid. Private transport services may similarly be able to dictate terms. Many co-operatives have been successful in providing transport over fixed routes for limited numbers of people. In general, however, they have failed to provide an effective transport service for widely dispersed customers with small and variable cargoes. Public sector transport services are often cheaper for the consumer, but they generally use large vehicles and tend to be operated only on a limited number of more important routes.

Commercial motor vehicle services are widely used for longer trips — indeed the demand often leads to overloading, frequent breakdowns and consequently unreliable service. The charge to the user varies considerably: with private services the price is often settled by negotiation, depending on the length of journey, the load being carried and the competition for business on the route. For all commercial services which use 'conventional' motor vehicles, unit charges tend to be higher for small loads and short trips.

... but other forms of transport are used ...

The main reason why few people own motor vehicles in developing countries (typical ownership levels are between 1 and 25 per 1000 people, compared with about 300 for the U.K. and over 600 for the U.S.A.), is simply that they cannot afford to buy them. Although these figures will increase, it is unlikely, given current trends in economic and population growth, that the situation will change significantly in the foreseeable future. Other types of vehicle are much more widely owned and used, however. These are very much cheaper to buy and operate; they are easier to manufacture, use and maintain; and many are capable of operating on narrow paths and unmade roads. If the literal meaning of 'vehicle' is used, i.e. including non-wheeled devices, they can be described as a range of 'basic vehicles'. This range includes aids to human porterage at one extreme, and basic versions of conventional motor vehicles at the other. Because of their relatively low purchase price they can also be described as 'low-cost'. The range covers many different types of vehicle, but the common characteristic is that they are all able to meet local needs — indeed many of them have evolved locally in response to these needs.

... to meet many needs.

The construction and operational characteristics of the complete range of low-cost vehicles are described in Part Two, but it is important to understand how widely they are used. Knowledge of this aspect is incomplete because only a limited number of surveys which have considered them as part of the transport system have been carried out, and many do

6

not normally appear in statistics for licensed or registered vehicles. The evidence that does exist, however, clearly indicates that they are the most common means of meeting the majority of everyday transport needs. The results of some of these studies are presented in Box C.

Box C   Availability and use of vehicles

- Surveys in Kenya (1971) showed that over 90 per cent of rural trips were on foot, 4 per cent by bicycle, with just 2 per cent by motorized transport.[8]

- A study in India (1977-8) showed that 74 per cent of households did not own any type of wheeled vehicle, nor did 89 per cent of households with less than 5 hectares of land. 17 per cent and 9 per cent respectively owned an animal cart or bicycle.[9]

- Another survey in India (1980) indicated that nearly 40 per cent of rural households spend no money on travel or transport.[10]

- A study in Malaysia (1981) reported 13 per cent of households as owning no wheeled vehicles, and a further 32 per cent as owning only a bicycle.[11]

- In a Nigerian study (1981) 32 per cent of the households owned an animal used for transport and 68 per cent a bicycle. About 27 per cent owned a motor cycle and 15 per cent other motor vehicles.[12]

- Evidence from the Philippines (1980) indicates that people who use commercial public transport have incomes at or above the median income level, i.e. the poorest travel little on these services.[13]

A wide range of vehicles exists ...

Eight broad categories of low-cost vehicles can be defined:

- Carrying aids;
- Wheelbarrows and handcarts;
- Animal transport;
- Pedal-driven vehicles;
- Motor cycles and conversions;
- Bicycle and motor cycle trailers;
- Basic motor vehicles;
- Agricultural vehicles.

These categories encompass a wide range of vehicles which cater for many different needs. The type of vehicles used vary according to transport requirements, as described previously, and to circumstances such as income level, topography, route conditions, climate, local resources and capabilities, and cultural traditions.

... but not all are widely available ...

Not all these vehicles are available

7

everywhere. In some places many of them are found; in others very few. Some are used only in one or two countries, and certain types are used in just one region within a country. Examples are given in Box D. Common sense indicates that the reason for this is not that the transport needs and social and economic circumstances of different countries or regions are so specialized that certain vehicles are appropriate there and nowhere else; instead it is much more likely that alternatives to the vehicles currently used are simply unknown to those who could exploit the knowledge.

Box D Uncommon but effective low-cost vehicles

● The *chee-geh*, a traditional load-carrying frame worn on the back, is believed to be unique to Korea. Its main advantage over other carrying aids is that it can be picked up and set down without assistance.

● The *Chinese wheelbarrow* is of quite different design from the wheelbarrow found in most other parts of the world. Scientific tests have proved it to be very effective, but it is rarely seen outside China.

● Two-wheeled handcarts are used to move goods by hand in many countries. They are particularly common in Indo-China, where they are also used as *bicycle trailers* to extend the range and speed of operation.

● The *motor cycle and sidecar* combination, which is a popular means of moving both goods and passengers in rural and urban areas of the Philippines, is found in very few other countries.

● A range of *motorized three-wheeled vehicles* has evolved on the island of Crete to meet the demand for a means of moving goods and people around farms and vineyards in the generally hilly terrain. They are also used by farmers as personal family transport, both locally and for longer trips into urban areas. They are especially useful at harvest time when many extra people are needed to work in the vineyards.

... and their potential has yet to be fully realised.

The lack of alternatives to existing vehicles is inevitably a major constraint on people's efforts to improve their methods of transport. People will only use a better method if it is both affordable and meets their needs. For many people, a graduated choice of efficient low-cost vehicles undoubtedly meets those criteria better than a limited range of much more expensive vehicles, yet these basic vehicles are not readily available to many who could make use of them.

Low-cost vehicles offer other benefits in addition to those felt by the user:

- they can be made by local manufacturers, using mainly local resources and materials;
- they minimize requirements for foreign exchange for initial purchase, fuel and spare parts; and
- they can provide useful employment in their manufacturing and maintenance, and in their use to provide transport services, at a low investment cost.

The benefits of using low-cost vehicles are thus felt by society as a whole, as well as by individuals. There is undoubtedly great potential in many countries for the provision and use of this type of transport – which has not yet been fully exploited

Benefits would result from improving transport ...

For the user, one or more of a number of benefits will result from using better methods of transport:

- less time or effort may be required to move a given load;
- labour or other operating costs may be reduced;
- journeys may be quicker, more comfortable or less expensive;
- transport bottlenecks may be relieved, which will reduce the delays and costs caused by transport not being available;

- the efficiency of other operations may be improved by making transport available at the right time and place; and
- other activities may be permitted to take place.

... by applying existing technology more widely ...

There is a variety of ingenious and efficient low-cost vehicles which are widely used in countries such as Indonesia, Malaysia, the Philippines and South Korea. Yet in many developing countries such vehicles are not used at all. In many cases improvements could be made by the transfer of efficient transport technologies from the countries where their utility has been proven to areas where they are unknown.

... by improving existing technology ...

Many low-cost vehicles are traditional devices which have remained unchanged for years. Almost all of them could be improved by applying contemporary technical knowledge, materials and manufacturing techniques so as to increase their efficiency and usefulness.

... and by developing new technology ...

Many low-cost vehicles are adaptations or conversions of other vehicles which were originally designed for a different purpose. In making improvements it is sometimes preferable to design a new vehicle from first principles rather than simply to make further modifications. The new vehicle will thus be based on the same concept as the existing one, but the detailed engineering will be different. Designing a vehicle, even a non-wheeled or non-motorized one, is far from straightforward. The result may appear simple, but it requires considerable engineering skill to make something which is simple and which works well. In this case 'simple' means that the vehicle is easy to operate and maintain, is attractive to the prospective owner, can be manufactured with minimum investment and can be sold at a competitive price. It is also important that the vehicle is designed to suit local market requirements and manufacturing resources. Some examples of the way in which equipment can be designed for local manufacture are given in Box E.

Designing the vehicle is only the first step towards successful manufacture however. Testing and market research; provision of adequate financial resources; and effective production, management and marketing methods, including making finance available for purchasers, will all play their part.

Box E   Design for local manufacture

In designing products to be manufactured and marketed in countries which have yet to establish a sophisticated and widespread industrial infrastructure, it is particularly important to take local circumstances into account. Materials and components which are already available locally should be utilized as far as possible, and the design should be capable of being manufactured with machinery and skills which already exist, or which can be obtained easily. In transferring technologies between countries it will be considerably easier and less expensive to adapt the design to suit the new circumstances, rather than attempt to change the circumstances to suit the design.

For example, one developing country in Asia imports hundreds of thousands of 40mm. diameter bearings for its large mining industry. These, and the corresponding steel shafts, are readily available at relatively low prices because of the large quantities imported. A vehicle rigidly designed around 25mm diameter bearings would be unable to take advantage of these cheap components, and the relatively small import quantities would almost certainly make them more expensive than the stock items.

In order to achieve successful small-scale production it is often important to rationalize the design by minimizing the number of different types and sizes of materials used to reduce purchasing and inventory costs and to minimize the fixed costs of manufacturing plant.

Box F Road development and prospects

• Even in a comparatively wealthy country such as Egypt, 32 per cent of villages are not provided with earth road access (1981); they are connected to larger villages, and thence the road network, only by footpaths.[14]

• In India (1978) about 70 per cent of villages do not have all-weather road connections, and 55 per cent are not connected to any type of road. Under current development plans the proportion of villages without an all-weather road connection will be reduced to 60 per cent by 1990 at a (1978) cost of US$ 3.5 billion.[15]

• According to the Pakistan Census of Agriculture (1980), nearly half of Pakistan's population lives eight kilometres or more away from a serviceable road link and is almost completely isolated during the rainy season. During the period 1978-83 a total of approximately 6,000km. of farm-to- market roads were added to the existing rural network of nearly 83,000km. It is estimated that as many as 160,000km. of farm- to-market roads are required to serve adequately a total of over 44,600 villages.[16]

Past efforts to improve transport ...

Most governments and aid agencies have always considered investment in transport to be an important priority. That investment has invariably been focussed on the construction of roads, particularly those designed to be used by cars and trucks. With construction costs of rural roads using conventional capital intensive methods of $50,000 per kilometre or more, even for so-called 'low-cost' roads, very large sums of money have been committed. Progress with the extension of the motorable road network has been correspondingly impressive, in terms of the number of kilometres constructed, but there is still a long way to go before the network will reach everyone. (see Box F).

... have not been focussed on the provision of vehicles.

As transport is a combination of road (of whatever quality) and vehicle it is surprising that more emphasis has not been placed on the provision of vehicles to complement the investment in roads. Presumably there has been an underlying assumption that private sector initiatives would take care of this. Evidently this has not happened to any great extent, and in many cases efforts to do so have been hampered by shortages of foreign exchange to pay for imported motor vehicles,

11

fuel and spare parts. In many of the photographs in Part Two people are to be seen carrying loads for long distances on motorable roads, presumably because more efficient vehicles which they could afford to use are not available.

Some countries have already begun to adopt a new approach.

The use of low-cost vehicles will undoubtedly be encouraged by government intervention and assistance. In two countries in particular, the People's Republic of China and the Socialist Republic of Vietnam, there has been formal recognition of the impossibility of putting sufficient investments into both roads and vehicles to make motorized transport available to a significant proportion of the population within a reasonable period of time. The dependence of most people on paths, tracks and traditional vehicles for most of their transport needs has been accepted, and considerable investments have been made in order to improve them, rather than replace them. A crucial part of this approach has been to produce certain technologically advanced items — such as bearings, pneumatic tyres, and components for spoked wheels and pedal drives — on a large scale in order to achieve acceptable quality at a reasonable price. These components are then incorporated into vehicles which can be manufactured by local communities on a small scale in order to meet their particular needs and resources. Further details of measures taken to promote low-cost transport in China and Vietnam are given in Box G.

Ideally, the starting point for the planning of transport improvements should be an analysis of the specific local-level transport needs of individual households or communities. The analysis should not be restricted to the needs of agricultural production, where so much attention is focussed at present, but should include the whole range of economic, social and other activities as well.

This analysis will allow the most effective measures for meeting these needs to be identified. These measures, which might include the introduction of suitable means of transport and provision of appropriate infrastructure will be aimed at improving the productivity of people's labour, and at enhancing the development of the community.

The purpose of this book is to suggest ideas ...

The information presented in Part Two is not intended to be an exhaustive listing of all the different forms of low-cost transport used in the developing world. Nor is it intended to provide detailed technical data about the vehicles. Rather its purpose is to highlight the diversity of methods, and the extent of their use, in order to suggest ways in which the transport facilities available to people might be improved more effectively in the future.

... to businessmen ...

These ideas represent a range of opportunities for entrepreneurs to

Box G   Low-cost transport in China and Vietnam

- *People's Republic of China*

In the 1950's local transportation administrations and local vehicle research instititutes were set up. Modern, large-scale plants were created
with the specific objective of producing ball bearings, axles, wheel components and pneumatic tyres, to enable local manufacturers to improve
the specification and performance of traditional wheelbarrows, handcarts
and animal carts.

In the 1960's animal-drawn carts were widely introduced to replace
manpower, and some non-motorized vehicles were replaced by motor
vehicles. Non-motorized vehicles remain important, however, because
they can be manufactured locally, they are not restricted to use on motorable roads and supplies of motor vehicles are limited.[17]

- *Socialist Republic of Vietnam*

The Government of Vietnam attaches special importance to the development of non-motorized vehicles. They are said to have advantages of zero
fuel consumption, high mobility, simplicity in manufacture and use, in-
frequent breakdown, low maintenance and repair costs, low investment
and high rate of return, and they can be used in different types of terrain
without large investments in road construction.

State enterprises manufacture axles, ball bearings and wheels which
are used in locally manufactured vehicles. Technical standards have been
defined for several different types of non- motorized vehicle and for the
construction of routes to suit them. The state also finances research into
methods of improving the quality and reliability of non-motorized vehicles.[18]

introduce new products for which a
ready market exists, and which
could form the basis of a successful
business. Where favourable conditions exist little non-commercial assistance should be necessary for the
business to become established, but
it is recognized that in many cases
government or aid agency intervention will be necessary in order to
stimulate commercial activity.

**... and to governments and aid
agencies.**

The kind of intervention needed
will vary according to circumstances,
but is likely to include:

- provision of technical and
  financial assistance to local
  vehicle manufacturers;
- creation of large-scale enter-

prises to manufacture critical components;

- provision of information and other assistance to encourage the transfer of successful technologies between countries;
- establishment of credit schemes for purchasers; and
- investment in the construction and improvement of the paths and tracks which can be used by low-cost vehicles and which are considerably less expensive to build than roads designed for 'conventional' motor vehicles.

PART TWO

THIS SECTION of the book describes a range of basic, or low-cost, vehicles which are relevant to the transport needs of many people in developing countries. They are divided into eight groups:

- Carrying aids
- Wheelbarrows and handcarts
- Animal transport
- Pedal-driven vehicles
- Motor cycles and conversions
- Bicycle and motor cycle trailers
- Basic motor vehicles
- Agricultural vehicles

Each group contains a number of distinct types of vehicle, and each type and its variations are described with the aid of photographs and, in a few cases, drawings. Each vehicle has different advantages and, of course, disadvantages, which make it more suitable for one purpose, or set of circumstances, than another. Many of the terms used in the descriptions such as 'advantage', 'disadvantage', 'large', 'small', etc., are necessarily relative, and the vehicles should therefore be assessed by the reader accordingly. In order to avoid repetition the introductions to the various groups provide an overall description and indicate characteristics relative to the other groups, whilst different vehicles within the groups are compared only with each other. Technical and operational details and geographical locations stated are correct to the author's knowledge.

The term 'load capacity' is used in the 'Remarks' section of the descriptions to define the weight the vehicle can carry.

Where it is undefined, the volume of the load is also included in the meaning.

The metric system of measurement is used throughout, although the centimetre (cm) is used in preference to the SI standard millimetre (mm) because it is more commonly used in general descriptions of this type. Engine power is expressed in (hp) which is more commonly used for this purpose than the SI standard kilowatt (kW).

Carrying aids

CARRYING AIDS enable people to carry loads on their head, shoulders or back. Their use allows people to move larger or heavier loads than can be carried by hand. Despite their apparent simplicity, carrying aids merit serious consideration because they are such an important means of transporting goods. They are easy to make and require little expenditure on materials, and are therefore widely affordable and (potentially) widely available. They can be used where difficult route conditions prevent the use of wheeled vehicles. Several types of carrying aid exist, with different characteristics which determine their convenience, suitability for a particular type of load or terrain, and safety.

Carrying aids provide a means of placing the load directly above the body's centre of gravity, either on the head, shoulders or high on the back. The weight is thus supported by the spine and legs as directly as possible, which minimizes the muscular effort required. With some aids the size and weight of load which one person can lift, unassisted, into the carrying position is less than the amount which can be carried. This is a significant disadvantage of these methods.

The International Labour Organization recommends (Recommendation 128, June 1967) than an adult male should carry maximum of 55kg., but many individual countries specify considerably lower maxima than this, especially for young people and women. Typically, loads carried in developing countries are in the range 25-30kg. The total weight of payload and carrying aid has an important effect on both speed and the distance which can be covered. Speed is limited to a walking pace of 4-5km/hr, and these methods are commonly used to carry loads for journeys of up to 20km. There are wide variations in the distance people are prepared to carry loads, however – depending on need, physical ability and the nature of the terrain.

Regular use of one type of aid develops special skills and strength in certain parts of the body. This physical conditioning is usually acquired during childhood, although it can be achieved quite quickly by an adult with frequent and regular practice.

Although carrying loads may appear to be a straightforward, if arduous, task, there are associated hazards. A report from Bangladesh indicates that fifty per cent of broken necks sustained there are the result of falls whilst carrying loads on the head. The habitual carrying and lifting of heavy loads over long periods of time can also result in damage to the spine, the joints, the muscles of the limbs and trunk, and to internal organs. In developing countries such injuries are particularly prevalent amongst women, on whom the burden of carrying loads very often falls.

Direct headloading

Women headloading maize to market along a main road. (WHO photo: E.Mandelman)

Description — pad of cloth to cushion the head, and container for the load if necessary.

Advantages — very simple and cheap.

Disadvantages — difficult to load without assistance;
— requires strength in the neck and considerable skill;
— load is unstable and difficult to control on steep or rough terrain;
— hazardous in the event of a fall.

Remarks This is probably the most widely used of all methods of carrying loads.

Headstrap (or tumpline)

Men carrying large loads of firewood to market using headstraps: Nepal. (FAO photo: S. Theuvenet)

Description   — loop of strong cloth or webbing, and container for the load if necessary.

Advantages   — very simple and cheap;
   — load is stable and easy to control.

Disadvantages   — difficult to load and unload without assistance; requires considerable skill, and strength in the neck;
   — stooped posture is likely to cause long-term back injuries;
   — hazardous in the event of a fall.

Remarks   Widely used on rough and steep terrain, and in crowded urban areas.

Shoulder strap

Woman carrying water in a plastic container using a shoulder strap: Ethiopia. Carrying water is frequently a time-consuming and arduous task for women in many countries. (WHO photo: M. de Vreede)

Description	— loop of strong cloth or webbing, and container for the load if necessary.
Advantages	— very simple and cheap;
	— load is stable and easy to control;
Disadvantages	— difficult to load and unload without assistance;
	— stooped posture likely to cause long-term back injuries.

Remarks A less common alternative to the headstrap.

Shoulder pole

Shoulder pole being used to carry a variety of goods in Bangladesh. The balance of the load can be adjusted by altering the position of the pole on the shoulder.

Description — section of bamboo or, less commonly, suitable timber, which tapers towards the ends. The load is suspended on rope, cane or bamboo hangers, either directly or in containers.

Advantages — simple and cheap;
— able to carry bulky or awkward loads;
— can be loaded and unloaded without assistance;
— shock loads imposed on the body by the vertical — oscillation of load are minimized by flexing of the pole;
— difficult to use on steep or rough terrain.

Disadvantages — skill required to prevent the load bouncing excessively;
— loads must be balanced.

Remarks Although apparently very simple, the shoulder pole is carefully shaped to make its natural frequency (rate of bounce), with an average load, about half the frequency of the rhythm of normal walking pace. This built-in suspension system reduces shock loads which would otherwise waste effort and cause discomfort. With loads that are smaller or greater than average, the natural frequency of the system is higher or lower respectively, and the user must either adjust his pace or alter the position of the loads. The shoulder pole is widely used in south-east Asia, and is also found in South America and in a few places in Africa.

Shoulder poles are sometimes used to carry unusually heavy loads by carrying one between two people, with the load suspended from the middle of the pole. Rigid poles can also be used; these are not as comfortable, but they are easier to make and the load does not have to be balanced.

A rigid shoulder pole in Laos. This type of pole is easy to make from bamboo or timber, but it is not as comfortable to use as a flexible pole. The load is balanced and controlled with one hand.

A shoulder pole in use on a fish farm in Indonesia. (UNA)

Two people using a shoulder pole for heavy load. (UNA)

The shoulder pole is well suited to awkward loads: India. (E.Hoddy)

Back frame

Description — Rectangular frame with shoulder straps which is carried on the back. The load is either tied directly on to the frame or contained in a basket or bag. The centre of gravity of the load should be high and as close to the back as possible. Modern pack frames are made of steel or aluminium tube with padded backs and shoulder straps. Heavier, less comfortable but much cheaper frames can be made from wood and rope or webbing. A hip belt may also be incorporated to transfer some of the weight directly to the legs.

Advantages — load is stable and easy to control.

Disadvantages — difficult to load and unload without assistance;
— modern versions are relatively expensive.

Remarks Although back frames are used by the military throughout the world, and for leisure use by civilians in industrialized countries, they are rarely seen elsewhere. One type of back frame which is used in a few developing countries has extended arms from which loads are suspended at each end. The user's hands can reach the load to limit the vertical movement, which makes this frame particularly suitable for carrying water or other liquids in open containers, and for irrigating or spraying crops.

A modern, aluminium back frame, with tensioned nylon webbing: U.K.

A simple wooden back frame with extended arms, used for carrying water in steep, narrow urban streets. (Used in this way, loading and unloading is not difficult): South Korea. (Earthscan photo: Mark Edwards)

Chee-geh

Description — an 'A' shaped back frame with extended legs such that it can be stood on the ground and supported with a stick for loading and unloading. When the frame is being carried the stick is used to aid walking. The traditional chee-geh is made from two strong, forked branches with woven straw back-padding and shoulder straps. The load container is made from woven sticks and may be lined with cloth or plastic to carry loose loads such as sand or earth.

Advantages — load is stable and easy to control.
— can be loaded and unloaded without assistance.

Disadvantages — relatively complicated and difficult to make.

Remarks   The chee-geh is believed to be unique to Korea, where it is indispensable for carrying loads up to fifty kilograms or more on mountain paths, and for negotiating streams and ditches which frequently cross farm roads.

An improved chee-geh has been made from steel tube, incorporating wheels which enable it to be used as a handcart on suitable terrain. The design was developed by Dr Seyeul Kim of Han Nam University with the close co-operation of farmers, to ensure that it was both practical and acceptable to the people who were intended to benefit from it.

A traditional wooden chee-geh: South Korea. (S. Kim)

Traditional chee-geh with load container of woven sticks: South Korea. (S. Kim)

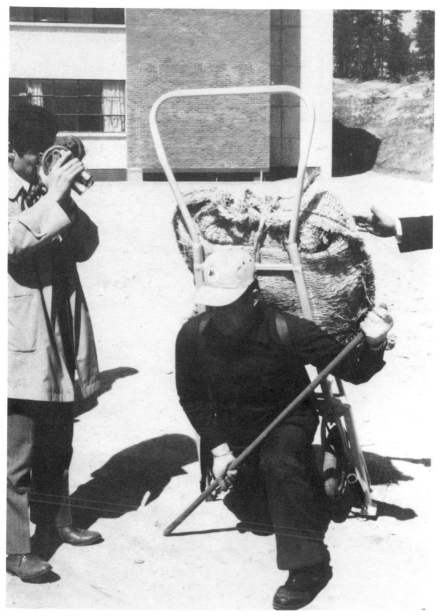

An improved chee-geh made of steel tube. The stick is an essential aid: South Korea. (S.Kim)

Another view of an improved chee-geh. The wheels fold down to convert the chee-geh into a handcart for use on suitable terrain.

Wheelbarrows and Handcarts

A WHEELED VEHICLE enables loads to be moved more efficiently than is possible with a carrying aid – and indeed they are essential when more than 50kg. has to be transported by one person in one trip. Less effort is needed to move a given load because most of the weight is supported by the wheel(s). However, on steep inclines a large proportion of the weight has to be supported by the operator, and on rough ground the rolling resistance of the vehicles may be high. The simplest and cheapest types of hand-propelled vehicles are wheelbarrows and handcarts.

Wheelbarrows have one wheel and are normally pushed. The operator must maintain balance and support part of the load – which limits the maximum load capacity. Wheelbarrows can be used to move loads along narrow paths and tracks where a wider vehicle could not go. A wheelbarrow may, however, have to be pulled over exceptionally large obstacles. Moving earth and other materials on construction sites is a long-standing use for wheelbarrows and their effectiveness when used in large numbers with good organization can be remarkable. The extensive railway networks built during the nineteenth century were constructed almost entirely with manual labour and non-motorized haulage methods, including animal-drawn carts and wheelbarrows. More recently, similar methods have been used to build large dams and canals in China.

Most handcarts have two wheels and may be pulled or pushed. Three or four wheels are sometimes used if a stable horizontal platform is needed. The operator doesn't have to support any of the weight if the cart is balanced by careful distribution of the load, and this means greater loads can be moved in one trip than when using a wheelbarrow – substantially greater when two or more people are employed. Handcarts are most useful on wide and level routes to carry large and heavy loads. On rough ground the higher dead weight of a handcart is a disadvantage.

The maximum load which can be moved with a wheelbarrow or handcart is determined by the roughness and gradient of the terrain, the strength and skill of the operator and the design of the vehicle. Large diameter wheels, pneumatic tyres and efficient bearings are desirable for low rolling resistance, and a lightweight but strong body will minimize the dead weight of the vehicle and hence maximize the payload. Maximum loads vary from about 100kg. for a Western wheelbarrow to over 1000kg. for a large handcart pulled by several people. Operating speed is, of course, generally limited to walking pace.

Western wheelbarrow

Two modern, western wheelbarrows. The pressed steel tray indicates that these wheelbarrows are probably mass-produced, but a folded and welded tray can be used for small-scale manufacture: Botswana.

The western wheelbarrow is best suited to short trips with frequent loading and unloading in work of the type shown here on a road construction site: Botswana.

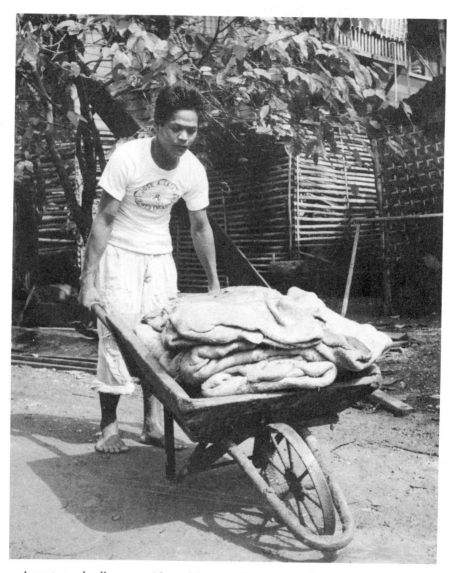

A western wheelbarrow with steel frame and wheel, and a wooden body. (UNA)

Description	— Modern designs consist of a steel tube frame with a sheet steel tray and a pneumatic or solid tyre 30-40cm in diameter (as shown). Variations exist to incorporate different materials and types of wheel, but the overall configuration is always very similar, with the load container well behind the wheel axle.
Advantages	— simple and robust;
	— light weight;
	— easy to load and unload;
	— stable and easy to manoeuvre.
Disadvantages	— small load capacity;
	— difficult to push over rough ground;
	— large proportion of the load supported by the operator, making it very arduous for long distance use;
	— has to be pulled backwards over large obstacles.

Remarks The Western wheelbarrow is most suitable for use on construction sites to move loose materials over short distances, with frequent loading and unloading. The maximum load is determined by the strength of the operator, but is normally about 100kg. It is widely used for construction work in most parts of the world.

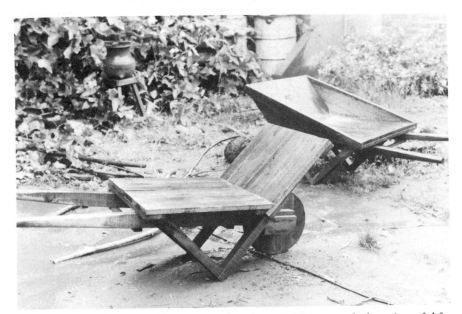

Two different western wheelbarrows made of wood. The open platform is useful for carrying loads in sacks or other containers; large loads can be tied on: Sudan.

Chinese wheelbarrow

A modern, steel, Chinese wheelbarrow with pneumatic tyre.

Description — The load container is located above, or sometimes either side of, a wheel about 70cm in diameter or more. Widely spaced handles help balance the load. Construction materials and details of the configuration vary, but the basic arrangement is always the same. Modern versions are shown, with steel tube and sheet bodies, spoked wheels, roller bearings and pneumatic tyres. A shoulder strap attached to the handles may be used to aid balancing, pushing uphill and braking downhill.

Advantages — small proportion of the load supported by the operator;
— large load capacity.

Disadvantages — high and unstable platform for loading;
— difficult to balance, especially when starting and stopping, because of high centre of gravity;
— hazardous if tipped over accidentally;
— load tends to slide out of container going over bumps;
— requires skill to handle effectively;
— legs tend to catch on obstacles and vegetation.

Remarks The Chinese wheelbarrow is best suited to transporting large loads over long distances, and is widely used in China for moving farm goods in rural areas. It is also used as an earth-moving wheelbarrow, often in very large numbers on major civil construction works. The maximum load is determined as much by the skill of the operator as by the strength of the vehicle, but is 150-200kg. This type of wheelbarrow is rarely seen outside China.

33

Chinese wheelbarrow with wooden frame. (Photo: J. Collett)

Chinese wheelbarrow with wooden frame used for moving farm goods. (Photo: J. Collett)

SFTV (Small farm transport vehicle)

An SFTV made of tubular steel and wood, with pneumatic tyre: U.K.

Description — A large diameter wheel, 50-60cm in diameter, is com- bined with a load platform or container either side of the wheel such that the centre of gravity of the load is low and just behind the axle. Widely spaced handles assist the operator in maintaining balance. Many different construction materials can be used, but a pneumatic tyre and tubular steel frame combination are preferred. A wide variety of general or special purpose bodies can be built on the basic frame. The version shown is most suit- able for carrying sacks, boxes and bulky goods, which can be tied on if required. A shoulder strap can be used to aid balancing, pushing uphill and braking downhill.

Advantages — small proportion of the load supported by the operator;
— large load capacity;
— easy to push over rough ground;
— easy to balance and manoeuvere.

Disadvantages — load needs to be balanced either side of wheel.

Remarks The SFTV is a new type of wheelbarrow which has been designed and developed by I.T. Transport Ltd and the Intermediate Technology Development Group. It is specifically intended to carry loads up to 150kg for distances of up to 10km, which are typical of the transport requirements of small farmers. It can be used on existing farm routes including rough and narrow paths and tracks, by unskilled people with minimal training. It has been designed to be manufactured by small scale industries in rural or urban areas, using locally available materials. Production costs will vary in different situations, but a selling price of half the price of a bicycle should be achievable. The basic design can be adapted readily for many different applications, primarily in agriculture but the SFTV may well be useful in urban areas as well. An extensive programme of prototype manufacture and field testing is being carried out in India before starting production and making the technology available to manufacturers elsewhere.

An SFTV with load containers for loose materials, made of steel angle and wood, shown with typical examples of a Chinese, and one Western, wheelbarrow.

Tubular steel SFTV carrying a 150kg load in sacks. Larger loads can be tied on. The handles are wide spaced to make it easier to balance the load. A simple shoulder strap can be added to provide further assistance.

Handcart

Lightweight wooden handcart with diameter wheels and pneumatic tyres: Laos.

Description — The most common handcart, as shown, has two wheels 70-150cm in diameter either side of a load platform. If a stable horizontal platform is required, a third wheel may be incorporated at one end, or four wheels may be used, two on each side. Brakes are desirable on large handcarts for parking and going downhill.

Advantages — large load capacity;
— small proportion of load is supported by the operator;
— does not need to be balanced;
— simple configuration permits easy adaptation for different applications;
— provides stable platform for loading and unloading.

Disadvantages — heavier than wheelbarrow;
— more expensive than wheelbarrow;
— cannot be used on narrow paths.

Remarks Most handcarts are normally operated by one person, but other people can help when required, either by pushing directly on the cart or by pulling with straps or ropes. Alternatively, an animal or a bicycle can be attached. In China it is common practice to hoist a simple sail on a handcart if the wind is blowing in the right direction. Load capacities vary from 150kg to about 1000kg, but 300kg is about the maximum for one operator. Handcarts are most commonly used in urban areas, often for street trading.

Handcart used for street trading: South Korea. (Photo: S. Kim)

Handcart used for transporting farm goods: South Korea. (Photo: S. Kim)

There are many types of handcart designed for various applications and made from different materials. Here is an industrial handcart made of steel with large diameter wheels and solid rubber tyres. This design allows the load to be tipped out: Philippines.

A traditional handcart made of wood and bamboo: India.

Handcart used for urban refuse collection: South Korea. (Photo: S. Kim)

41

A lightweight four-wheeled cart used as a mobile stall for street trading: India.

Some handcarts can be hitched to a small animal, such as a donkey: China.

A small handcart can also be used as a bicycle trailer to increase the speed and range of operation: Laos.

Several empty handcarts being towed by an animal cart: China.

Animal transport

Riding donkeys to market: Haiti. (WHO photo: F. Mattioli)

IN MANY PARTS of the world domesticated animals, such as mules, donkeys, horses, oxen (particularly bullocks and buffaloes) and camels, are used in a variety of ways to transport both people and goods. Although these forms of transport are slow, generally being restricted to the walking pace of the animal, much greater loads can be moved than is possible with human power alone. Animals can move over any terrain where it is possible to walk, so they may be the only alternative to human porterage in areas where the conditions or routes are unsuitable for wheeled vehicles.

There is a long history of the use of animals for transport. In Europe and North America, horses and horse-drawn vehicles formed a substantial and essential part of both the rural and urban transport system until motor vehicles became widely available in the early part of this century. In many countries in Asia, animal-drawn carts continue to carry a large proportion of the total goods moved, especially in rural areas within and around farms and villages. Some 15 million carts are estimated to exist in India alone. Although some attempts have been made to improve the efficiency of traditional animal transport, little has yet been achieved. There remains considerable potential both for improving traditional methods, and for introducing the concept and means to areas where they are unknown at present. This potential is clearly particularly good where animals are already in use for other agricultural activities.

Animals can be ridden as a means of personal transport, with little or no equipment needed other than some means of keeping control. This may be no quicker than walking, but it is much less arduous. Loads can be carried on an animal's back using a saddle and a pack or pannier to position the load. To carry heavier loads, at least part of the weight must be supported by the ground rather than the animal. The simplest way of doing this is to use a sledge, which is easily made from a variety of materials at very little cost. The greatest load-carrying capacity is achieved by harnessing the animal, or several animals, to a two or four-wheeled cart.

The draught, or pulling, power available is determined by the type, breed and condition of the animal. The efficiency with which this power is used depends on the 'dead' weight of the vehicle or pannier, the way in which the animal is harnessed or loaded, and, in the case of carts, the rolling resistance of the vehicle.

The successful and efficient use of animals for transport is dependent to a large extent on how well they are managed, particularly with regard to care and training. If draught animals are to be introduced to people who have not previously used this form of power, time and training will be needed for them to acquire the necessary skills. It is also important to remember that animals consume fuel in the form of food whether or not they are working.

Animal panniers

General purpose wooden panniers: Ethiopia.

Description — Animal panniers take many different forms, but the two essential features are a saddle (which may simply be layers of cloth) to distribute the load and protect the animal, and a load container with straps to hold it in position. General purpose panniers may be in the form of a wooden frame, as shown, or they may be rope, cloth, wickerwork or leather bags or baskets. Special purpose panniers can be made for specific tasks, such as the transport of water.

Advantages — very simple and cheap;
— can be used on narrow paths and steep, rough terrain;
— can be made by the user, or by local craftsmen.

Disadvantages — limited load capacity.

Remarks Load capacities vary, according to the type of animal, from about 150kg for a donkey to 400kg for a camel. Panniers are commonly used with horses, mules, donkeys and camels, especially in mountainous parts of the world. There is little evidence of the use of oxen, although buffalo are used to carry people.

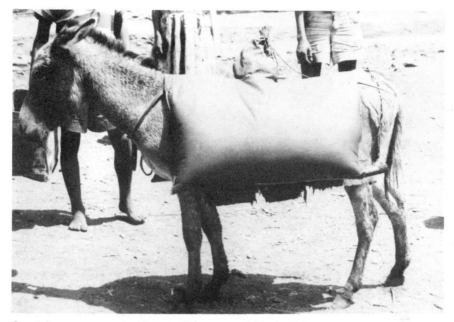

Special purpose panniers for carrying water: Ethiopia. These panniers are made from a large rectangle of canvas, folded in half and sewn around the edge with a simple filling spout in the middle and drain plugs in two corners.

A team of donkeys with very low-cost panniers (made of hessian sacks) being used to move construction materials in an urban area: India.

47

Animal sledge

A buffalo sledge being used to move 200kg of fertilizer: Philippines.

Description	— sledges usually consist of an open frame made of wood or bamboo with a yoke or other simple harness to attach the animal. A strong, light structure is desirable, the runners being wide to stop them digging into the ground.
Advantages:	— simple and cheap;
	— can be manufactured by the user, or by local craftsman.
Disadvantages	— inefficient use of draught power because of friction between the sledge and the ground;
	— rapid wear of runners;
	— cannot be used on narrow paths;
	— may cause erosion of earth roads and tracks by forming ruts which become channels for water.

Remarks: Although sledges are not as efficient as carts, they are considerably cheaper and easier to make. As panniers often cannot be used with oxen, a sledge may be the only way that small farmers can afford to use an ox for transport. Load capacities vary greatly according to the type of animal and the route surface, but are typically about fifty percent greater than can be carried with panniers.

Sledges are used in only a few countries. In at least one, where the erosion of earth roads by the uncontrolled flow of rainwater is a serious problem, they are illegal.

A closer view of the lightweight buffalo sledge shown above: Philippines.

Ox sledge: Botswana. Even in a device as simple as a sledge there is scope for the improvement of traditional designs. Contrast the heavy, inflexible construction with the Philippine buffalo sledge.

49

Animal cart

A traditional bullock cart being used to transport wood: Bangladesh.

Description: — A wide variety of carts exists, designed for different purposes, made from various materials and adapted to suit different types and sizes of animal. The most common design has two wheels, 70 - 150cm in diameter, one either side of a load platform. The centre of gravity of the load is positioned just in front of the axle so that the animal supports only a small proportion of the load. Traditional carts are made of wood or bamboo, with large diameter wheels to give low rolling resistance. Pneumatic tyres and roller bearings may be incorporated into otherwise traditional designs in order to further reduce rolling resistance, and hence increase load capacity. This is often achieved by using a scrap motor vehicle axle. Modern designs have lightweight steel frames and may incorporate a simple suspension system and brakes for efficiency, comfort and safety. To carry heavier loads, or if a stable, horizontal platform is required, a four-wheeled cart may be used. These carts usually incorporate suspension, or have a single backbone which will twist, to avoid imposing excessive stress on the cart when only one wheel passes over a bump. A four-wheeled cart has to have a steering mechanism, which adds weight and complexity. Special purpose carts can be made for specific tasks, such as transporting water or construction materials.

Advantages: — can carry large and heavy loads;
— simple configuration permits easy adaptation for different purposes.

Disadvantages: — narrow wheels of traditional carts may damage earth roads;
— relatively expensive compared to other animal transport;
— cannot operate on narrow paths;
— four-wheeled carts have a large turning circle.

Remarks: The draught power available from the animal varies according to species, but more than one animal can be used if required. The gain in useful power is not directly proportional to the number of animals however, and it is not normally worth using more than four. Maximum loads can therefore vary widely from about 500-3000kg. Pneumatic tyres and roller bearings have a very significant effect on the performance of a cart by reducing rolling resistance, on both hard and soft ground. Load capacity can be increased by up to 100% compared with an equivalent traditional cart, albeit at greater cost. A number of organizations manufacture pneumatic-tyred wheel/axle assemblies specifically designed for use with animal carts. Standard motor vehicle wheels are often used to simplify the supply of original components and spare parts. Scrap tyres may be fitted since a tread is not necessary on a cart. Complete wheel/axle assemblies from scrap motor vehicles are less satisfactory, as they are unnecessarily heavy and replacement parts may be difficult to find.

A wooden cart incorporating pneumatic tyres: China.

For all types of cart, a harness which is comfortable and which fits the animal properly is essential to produce maximum effort and to prevent the formation of sores. Many different types of harness exist, which vary according to the type of cart, the species and number of animals used, and local preference. A detailed description of these is beyond the scope of this book, but further information is contained in *The Harnessing of Draught Animals* by Ian Barwell and Michael Ayre (I T Publications, London 1982)

Modern steel carts used for construction work: Botswana.

A lightweight cart with suspension for carrying passengers: Ethiopia.

Purpose-built wheel/axle assemblies, with pneumatic tyres and efficient bearings, can be made by specialist manufacturers.

Four-wheeled carts have a large capacity but they are difficult to manoeuvre: Botswana.

A tipping mechanism saves a significant amount of time in unloading loose materials, which is important in construction work: Botswana.

A camel is strong enough to pull a four-wheeled cart on its own. A set of spare parts as comprehensive as this is not normally necessary! Pakistan.

54

The efficiency of traditional carts can be increased by fitting a new wheel/axle assembly with pneumatic tyres: India.

Four-wheeled carts are best suited to use on wide, level routes with large loads: India.

Pedal-driven vehicles

PEDAL-DRIVEN bicycles and tricycles were developed in Europe in the second half of the nineteenth century. The configuration of the bicycle which is so familiar today became the standard design in the early part of the twentieth century, after an intensive period of development. Since then bicycles have remained popular as a means of personal transport throughout the world, and significant innovations in bicycle design have occurred in industrialized countries to cater for the demand for different leisure uses. These innovations have been of only limited relevance to the ways in which bicycles are used in developing societies, and the design of these bicycles has changed little.

The utility of pedal-driven vehicles extends beyond personal transport to the movement of goods and passengers. This has long been recognized and cycles are widely used for this purpose in many developing countries. Most of these load-carrying cycles are adaptations of standard bicycles. Wheels, forks and frames are strengthened and load frames added. A load platform and third wheel may be added to form a sidecar, and tricycles are made by removing the front or rear half of the bicycle and replacing it with a two-wheeled body. The wheels on three- wheeled cycles, unlike bicycle wheels, are subjected to side loads when turning and going across slopes and must therefore be stronger than bicycle wheels. Improved brakes and multi-speed gears, though desirable on load-carrying cycles, are rarely used. A wide variety of pedal-driven load carriers exists, but there remains considerable scope for the development of bicycles and tricycles specifically designed for this purpose.

A pedal-driven vehicle uses human effort about four times more efficiently than walking. This enables a person to travel faster (about three times walking speed) and/or to carry a greater load. However the performance of pedal-driven vehicles is much more sensitive to route conditions and gradients than walking. Load capacity is determined by the strength of construction, the 'dead' weight of the vehicle and the physical condition of the rider. Pedalling more than 200kg (including the load but excluding the rider) is slow and arduous, however, except on very smooth and flat terrain.

The cash cost of purchasing pedal-driven vehicles varies widely but a standard bicycle is normally about the same price as a medium-sized handcart, whereas a load-carrying tricycle costs two to three times as much.

Bicycle

A standard 'roadster' bicycle with a small load frame and parking stand: China. (Photo: J. Collett)

Description	— Modern bicycles in industrialized countries have a variety of frame configurations for different applications, and use lightweight components and multi-speed gears. The most popular bicycle in developing countries is the heavyweight 'roadster', of rugged construction with wide tyres, designed for reliability on rough roads without the need for frequent maintenance. A parking stand and a small load rack are often incorporated.
Advantages	— can be used on narrow and rough paths; — relatively light; — cheaper than load-carrying cycles; — able to manoeuvre through congested urban traffic.
Disadvantages	— limited load capacity.

Remarks Although standard bicycles are intended to carry the rider only, a passenger may be carried on the load rack. If a large or awkward load has to be carried, or in order to negotiate a very rough or steep section of a route, the bicycle can always be pushed rather than ridden.

A passenger can be carried on the load frame of a standard bicycle: Laos.

To carry large loads, bicycles can be pushed rather than ridden: Indonesia.

Load-carrying bicycle

A strengthened bicycle with a load frame can carry a substantial load. This one is carrying 200kg of cassava: Indonesia.

Description	— A standard heavyweight 'roadster' bicycle can be modified for carrying loads by strengthening the original construction and adding a load frame. Thicker spokes and hubs with bigger axles may be incorporated into the back wheel, extra struts may be added to the front forks, and the main frame may be strengthened with additional tubes. Loads are usually carried either side of the back wheel on a pannier frame, to which they can be attached directly or contained in bags, sacks or baskets. Special-purpose panniers can be made for specific loads such as water or milk containers. To accommodate larger loads, the bicycle frame may be lengthened and a long, wide rack may be fitted, which is especially useful for carrying boxes. Some load-carrying bicycles incorporate a small front wheel so that a large load container can be fitted above it.
Advantages	— can be used on narrow paths; — can be used for personal transport as well as carrying goods; — lighter and cheaper than three-wheeled cycles.
Disadvantages	— difficult to balance, especially with high and heavy loads and at low speed; — poor braking when loaded, especially in wet conditions.

Remarks The maximum load capacity is dependent on the extent of strengthening modifications, and can vary from 50 - 200kg. Load-carrying bicycles are especially common in the Far East.

Large load containers can be fitted to a standard bicycle: China. (Photo: J. Collett)

These bicycles have been heavily modified and strengthened for load carrying. The strengthening of the front forks may look excessive, but if the front forks break, this can lead to serious injury. The gloves are used in very cold weather: South Korea. (Photo: S. Kim)

A side view of the bicycle shown above. Five 25kg boxes of apples are being carried: South Korea. (Photo: S. Kim)

Two bicycles with 200kg of cassava (see photo above) being moved 30km from farm to market: Indonesia.

Purpose-built, load-carrying bicycle – with a parking stand and a load frame at the front and rear – used for postal deliveries: Switzerland.

A similar type of bicycle to the one shown above, but the frame construction is very different: Switzerland.

'Low-gravity' carrier bicycle: a traditional British design, also found in Africa.

Another British design of carrier bicycle with a load frame in front: Zimbabwe.

64

Bicycle and sidecar

A bicycle and sidecar is well suited to carrying long loads: Indonesia.

Description — A load platform with a third wheel can be fixed to a bicycle to form a sidecar, so that the load is spread between all three wheels. The frame, wheels and forks are usually strengthened to accommodate the load. To minimize side loads on the wheels, the load platform is as low as possible.

Advantages — can be used on poor roads which have two wheel tracks;
— can be used to carry very long loads (see photo);
— stable platform easy to load and unload;
— cheap and simple conversion compared with tricycles.

Disadvantages — cannot operate on narrow paths;
— unstable when lightly loaded;
— very poor braking when loaded, especially in wet conditions.

Remarks Maximum load capacity depends on the strength of construction, and can vary from 150 - 300kg. Sidecars are found in only a few countries. The relative simplicity of adding a sidecar to an existing bicycle and the need to modify the details of the design to suit different makes and sizes of bicycle, offers good potential for manufacture by individual metalworkers or co-operatives.

A weatherproof passenger compartment fitted to a bicycle and sidecar provides an effective means of family transport: China. (Photo: J. Collett)

A bicycle and sidecar can also be used to carry adult passengers: Burma.

Tricycle with front load platform

A tricycle with a load platform in front. A low platform is good for stability and strength: Mexico.

Description	— Most tricycles of this type are made by replacing the front half of a load-carrying bicycle with a two-wheeled load platform incorporating a steering mechanism. The front wheels are strengthened to accommodate side loads, but further modifications are not normally necessary. A parking brake is sometimes added for convenience.
Advantages	— easy to load and unload; — load platform can be very low to minimize side loads.
Disadvantages	— cannot operate on narrow paths; — difficult to steer, especially when loaded; — large loads and passenger protection restrict driver's vision; — very poor braking when loaded, especially in wet conditions.

Remarks: This type of tricycle, known as a *becak* in Indonesia, can be adapted for carrying goods or passengers. They are often used as mobile market stalls because the rider can see the load and does not necessarily have to dismount to serve customers. Load capacities vary from 150-300kg. They are used in several countries, including Indonesia, Malaysia and Mexico.

Tricycles of different types provide an effective taxi service in many urban areas. These are 'becaks' – which have seats in front – in Indonesia.

A tricycle can be used as a mobile market stall, with an enclosed display cabinet if required: Malaysia.

Tricycle with rear load platform

Tricycle with a general-purpose load platform at the rear: Thailand.

Description — Most tricycles of this type are made by replacing the rear half of a load-carrying bicycle with a two-wheeled load platform incorporating a drive mechanism. Usually only one rear wheel is driven and the other is allowed to turn freely. The rear wheels are usually strengthened to accommodate side loads. A parking brake may also be added.

Advantages — large, versatile load platform;
— easy to load and unload.

Disadvantages — cannot operate on narrow paths;
— very poor braking when loaded, especially in wet conditions.

Remarks   This type of tricycle is known as a *rickshaw* in India and Bangladesh, where it is widely used in urban and rural areas for carrying goods or passengers. In China and other countries of the Far East a dual-purpose load platform is often added for carrying both goods and passengers. Load capacities vary from 150-300kg.

Tricycles are useful in urban and rural areas. This one is being used to move farm goods in Bangladesh. The construction is very similar to the passenger rickshaw shown below.

The narrow raised platforms and uprights at the side are useful for carrying large loads, or to provide seats for passengers: Laos.

(Top) A passenger rickshaw in a rural area of Bangladesh.
(Left) Passenger rickshaws provide an effective taxi service in many urban areas in India and Bangladesh.

71

Oxtrike

Oxtrike with a general purpose load container: U.K.

Description — The Oxtrike is a modern tricycle which is specifically designed for carrying loads. The frame is made of square steel tube for strength without excessive weight. Foot-operated brakes with a parking lock act on both rear wheels. The load platform is low, to minimize side loads, and has springs underneath. 50cm diameter wheels with wide tyres are used, and a standard three-speed gearbox and differential drive can be fitted if required. A variety of general or special purpose bodies can be fitted.

Advantages — relatively light;
— good brakes;
— large, versatile load platform;
— easy to load and unload;
— optional gearbox improves efficiency;
— optional differential improves handling, especially in wet conditions.

Disadvantages — not widely available;
— cannot operate on narrow paths.

Remarks The Oxtrike has been developed by IT Transport Ltd. from an original concept of Stuart Wilson of Oxford University. It can be manufactured on a small scale with minimum capital investment, using widely available materials and components. Load capacity is the same as for other tricycles. The Oxtrike is currently in production in Kenya.

Tricycles such as the Oxtrike are well suited to the distribution of goods to small retailers in urban areas: Kenya.

The design of the Oxtrike can be adapted to suit locally-available materials and manufacturing resources. Contrast the design of this vehicle, made in Kenya, with the U.K. version above.

Motor cycles and conversions

MOTOR CYCLES have been developed since about 1900 to meet the demand in industrialized countries for a quick and effortless means of personal transport. Since the early 1960's the international motor cycle market has become dominated by lightweight machines manufactured in Japan, where the economies of efficient, large-scale production have kept their cost to a modest level. Evidently, they are widely affordable and effective, especially for travelling in congested urban areas. Their use in many industrialized countries is constrained by frequent bad weather and the safety hazards of riding a motor cycle on busy roads. Motor cycles are also popular in developing countries, particularly as a means of personal and family transport in urban areas. Because of their relatively high cost, however, they are beyond the means of many people.

The potential utility of motor cycles for moving more than two people, or substantial loads, is undoubtedly good, although few motor cycles designed specifically for this purpose have yet been produced by the major manufacturers. However, standard motor cycles and components are converted into load-carrying vehicles by small-scale enterprises in some countries. The scope of these conversions ranges from simply fitting a pannier frame to creating a three or four-wheeled vehicle, and there are wide variations in performance and cost.

Although these vehicles are generally more expensive to buy than non-motorized vehicles, they have important advantages. Physical effort is reduced or eliminated, and the speed of operation is substantially higher. The load capacity may be no larger, but much greater distances can be covered, more trips can be made in a given amount of time and hills do not present a serious obstacle.

Motor-assisted cycle

Description   — A small (35-50cc) petrol engine can be added to a pedal-driven vehicle in order to provide assistance. The drive arrangement may be either direct to the tyre or incorporated into the existing transmission. The normal pedal drive is retained so that the engine provides assistance, rather than the sole means of power. In order to with-

A small petrol engine can be added to a strengthened bicycle to increase the speed and range of operation: South Korea. (Photo: S. Kim)

A small engine can also be added to a tricycle - in this case a passenger rickshaw in India.

stand the increased loads imposed on it by the engine the original vehicle needs to be of rugged construction. Critical components such as forks and wheels can be strengthened, and brakes upgraded.

Advantages — cheap method of increasing the utility of an existing vehicle;

— low fuel consumption;

— simple to maintain.

Disadvantages — strength, durability and performance of vehicle components not designed for increased power;

— possibly high running costs caused by frequent replacement of parts.

Remarks Although the load capacity of the original vehicle will not be increased, the speed will be considerably higher (up to 30km/hr), especially in hilly areas. These vehicles are quite common in countries where suitable engines are available, but they are not usually as popular as purpose-built motor cycles. There is increasing interest in the industrialized countries in the use of electric motors to assist pedal cycles.

Rear view of a motor-assisted cycle rickshaw: India.

Motor cycle

Motor cycle with weatherproof load container: Zimbabwe.

Description — Many different types and sizes of motor cycle exist, but all of them have large wheels (50-70cm in diameter), with an exposed engine and chain drive. The most popular have engine sizes in the range 50-250cc. Adaptations for load carrying can be a simple pannier frame, to which loads are tied directly, or they may consist of a large, weatherproof box as illustrated. These fittings are usually attached to the small rear luggage rack which is a standard feature on most motor cycles.

Advantages — fast and convenient means of personal transport;
— load-carrying attachments easily fitted;
— can be used on narrow paths and rough terrain;
— able to manoeuvre through congested urban traffic.

Disadvantages: — limited load capacity;
— difficult to balance when loaded.

Remarks The motor cycle is primarily intended for personal transport. Although considerable weights can be carried (up to 150kg), the volume of the load is restricted by the difficulty of balancing it, especially on rough ground. The motor cycle excels as a fast urban delivery vehicle carrying small goods and documents, whilst purpose-built 'trail bikes' can travel over remarkably steep and rough routes.

Surprisingly large loads can be carried on a motor cycle with a suitable load frame and careful packing. However, a load as large as this would be difficult to control on rough ground or busy streets.

A motor cycle is the only type of motorized transport that can travel on narrow footpaths, which are often the sole access route to rural settlements: Indonesia.

Scooter

Scooters are useful for carrying small loads in rural areas.

Description — Only a limited range of scooters exists, their main characteristics being a sheet steel body, small wheels (approximately 40cm in diameter), an enclosed engine and direct drive to the rear wheel. Engine sizes vary from 50-200cc. Load-carrying adaptations may consist of a pannier frame or weatherproof box fixed to a rear luggage rack.

Advantages — cleaner to ride and quieter than motor cycle;
— low centre of gravity makes balancing easier at low speed;

Disadvantages — limited load capacity;
— difficult to fit load-carrying attachments;
— poor performance on rough ground because of small wheels and low ground clearance;
— more difficult to balance at high speed than motor cycle (because of small wheels).

Remarks Scooters are mainly used in urban areas where they are a popular means of personal transport in many countries. They originated in Italy and are still manufactured in very large numbers there, and under licence elsewhere, notably in India.

79

Motor cycle and sidecar

Description — A tubular steel sidecar is fitted to the side of a motor cycle of engine size 100cc or more. The motor cycle frame is normally strengthened and modified for this purpose. Most sidecars can be used for carrying goods or people, although some have a simple flat platform for goods only.

Advantages — high ground clearance and large wheels give good performance on rough ground;
— can be used on poor roads which have two wheel tracks;
— light enough to be pushed over (or around) very bad or wet sections of road;
— large load capacity;
— relatively cheap and simple conversion of standard motor cycle;
— easy to load and unload.

Disadvantages — poor braking;
— unstable with light loads when turning.

Remarks These vehicles are widely used in parts of South East Asia, notably the Philippines where some 70,000 are estimated to be in use. They are a remarkably versatile and effective means of low-cost motorized transport for both rural and urban use. Payloads and speeds depend on the strength of construction and size of the engine, but 500kg or six passengers are commonly carried at up to 60km/hr. They are normally used on a 'for hire' basis.

Motor cycle and sidecar used for carrying passengers: Indonesia.

Motor tricycle

A motor tricycle used as an urban taxi: India.

Description — A standard motor cycle or scooter can be converted into a tricycle by replacing either the front or the rear wheel with a two-wheeled load platform, in the same way as a pedal-driven tricycle. The bodywork may be totally enclosed for carrying goods or passengers (as shown), or it may be a flat platform for goods only.

Advantages — driver and load may be protected from weather;
— stable;
— large load capacity;
— easier to load and unload;
— greater load area than sidecar;

Disadvantages — heavier, and requires larger engine than sidecar;
— relatively complicated and expensive.

Remarks   Load capacity is about the same as for a motor cycle and sidecar. A simpler conversion, which looks very similar to a tricycle, can be made by placing a two-wheeled load platform and bodywork behind a complete motorcycle, to create a four-wheeled vehicle (see photo). The resulting vehicle has characteristics similar to a motor tricycle.

A four-wheeled motor cycle conversion: Philippines.

A scooter can also be converted into a motor tricycle. This type has a weatherproof passenger compartment.

Bicycle and motor cycle trailers

BICYCLE TRAILERS, and to a lesser extent motor cycle trailers, have been used for many years in certain parts of Europe as a convenient, simple and cheap means of transporting loads in both urban and rural areas. Yet, with certain isolated exceptions, cycle trailers have not been used to any significant extent in developing countries. They are found in parts of West and Southern Africa, and in Indo-China, but in few other places.

A trailer has several important characteristics as a load carrier. It enables a standard bicycle or motor cycle to carry substantial loads with minimal modifications, yet the trailer can be attached or removed quickly and easily. The towing vehicle can be used on its own for small loads or for personal transport, and the trailer attached as and when needed for carrying larger loads (or possibly passengers). The trailer can also be used on its own as a small handcart. Someone with a small income can purchase a bicycle or motor cycle, and at a later date buy a trailer to extend the utility of the vehicle. A trailer would normally cost beween one third and half the price of a bicycle or motor cycle. The potential for the use of trailers is particularly good in countries where cycles are already widely used.

A well-designed trailer will minimize the additional loading on the cycle frame, but the total weight of the load and trailer should not exceed that of the vehicle and rider – about 100kg for a bicycle or 250kg for a motor cycle. Excessive loads can make the combination unstable, and the cycles brakes are not likely to be powerful enough for safe control. The hitch must allow the trailer to move relative to the towing vehicle (when turning or going over bumps), but at the same time transfer a steady pulling or braking force to it without 'snatching', and be easy to connect and disconnect. A two-legged parking stand fitted to the cycle will make loading and unloading easier.

Probably the best example of the successful commercial use of cycle trailers is in Switzerland where they are widely used for postal deliveries. Despite high wage rates, hilly terrain and frequent poor weather they are used as a *cost-effective* means of transport, which is fast, flexible and convenient to operate. Bicycles and trailers originally proved the viability of the system but these have now been largely superseded by small motorcycles and trailers. (Details of the system are given in D. Weightman's report on design and use of bicycles, mopeds and trailers by the Swiss Post Office in Geneva - I. T. Transport Ltd., 1980).

Further information about the construction of trailers and hitches for bicycles is contained in *The Design of Cycle Trailers* by I. J. Barwell (I T Publications, London 1977).

Two-wheeled bicycle trailer

Bicycle trailer used for delivering bread: Zimbabwe.

Description — A bicycle trailer consists essentially of a load container with one wheel either side, such that the centre of gravity of the load is just in front of the axle line. The hitch is usually fixed to the bicycle frame above the rear wheel, or sometimes on one side of the rear hub. Large wheels (50-70cm in diameter) and pneumatic tyres are preferred for use on rough ground, but small wheels (30-40cm in diameter) are adequate in urban areas. A strong but light construction will minimize the 'dead' weight of the vehicle. A wide variety of general or special purpose load containers may be fitted.

Advantages — cheap and simple.

Disadvantages — cannot be used on narrow paths;
— must be loaded carefully when hitched to the bicycle to prevent tipping.

Remarks A problem common to all conventional two-wheeled trailers is that they are difficult to use on poor roads which have two distinct wheel tracks. This can be overcome by using an 'offset' trailer, which is towed to one side so that one wheel is in line with those of the bicycle. This technique has been developed by IT Transport and has surprisingly little effect on performance or handling. Another method is to use a trailer with a single wheel which follows the same line as the bicycle. The trailer and hitch must be carefully designed to make the combination stable.

A notable special-purpose trailer is the bicycle ambulance, adapted by IT Transport and Intermediate Technology Industrial Services from an original version used in Malawi.

Load-carrying bicycle and trailer used for postal deliveries in Switzerland. This is a cost-effective means of transport despite high wage rates, hilly terrain and poor weather. This trailer can also be used as a handcart and has independent brakes.

A 'bicycle ambulance' can be used to carry patients to a health centre or hospital when other means of transport are not available. The bicycle ambulance can be hitched behind any bicycle (no special hitch fitting is needed). The stretcher is removable. This trailer was developed in the U.K. by I.T. Transport Ltd., from an original design used in Malawi.

(Top) A single-wheeled trailer is useful for carrying loads on narrow footpaths, which are often the only access route to rural settlements. The configuration of the trailer and the design of the hitch are critical for satisfactory handling and performance. This trailer was designed and developed by I.T. Transport Ltd. in the U.K.

(Left) Rear view of bike and trailer.

Bicycle trailers are used in only a few developing countries. This general purpose trailer was made in Malawi.

This general purpose trailer is being developed for manufacture in India, with the assistance of I. T. Transport Ltd. There are about 25 million bicycles in India, but trailers are almost unknown.

Two wheeled motor cycle/scooter trailer

Urban delivery trailer with weatherproof, fibreglass, load container: Zimbabwe.

Description	— The basic arrangement of a motor cycle/scooter trailer is the same as that of a bicycle trailer, although the construction is stronger to accommodate higher speeds and larger loads. Large diameter wheels are preferred for use on rough ground, and pneumatic tyres are essential. Suspension is desirable to minimize the effect of the trailer on the handling of the motor cycle. A ball and socket-type hitch is usually used and attached to the rear luggage rack. The strength and load capacity of trailers and hitches vary to suit different sizes of motor cycle.
Advantages	— large load capacity.
Disadvantages	— requires skill to operate safely.

Remarks   A different system of hitching a trailer to a scooter has been developed in India. The hitch is fitted in front of the seat and slides on the trailer arm to allow the scooter to turn.

In some countries the use of motor cycle trailers has been prevented by law, but this situation is likely to change in the near future. This should encourage their emergence as an important means of low-cost motorized transport, because of their potential for increasing the utility of *existing* vehicles.

88

Small motor cycles and trailers are used by the Swiss Post Office to complement the use of bicycles and trailers. The motor cycle trailers are similar in design, but the construction is more robust and a simple suspension is used.

A scooter can also be used to pull a trailer, although the arrangement of the hitch is relatively complicated. This type was developed in India, but is shown on test in Sri Lanka.

A small motor cycle and trailer can carry a surprising amount of goods and passengers, although loading like this is not common or recommended. (Photo: Terry Fincher)

Small motor cycle and general purpose trailer.

Basic Motor Vehicles

THE TERM 'basic motor vehicle' is used to describe a range of light goods or passenger vehicles which are less sophisticated than conventional cars, vans or trucks. They are an attractive prospect for manufacturing in developing countries because there is a comparatively low investment required for production facilities and equipment, and because a high proportion of local labour and materials can be incorporated. They are attractive to the user because they are usually less expensive to buy than conventional imported vehicles; spare parts should be easily obtainable; and, with a small engine and straightforward mechanical arrangement, they are relatively cheap to run and easy to maintain. There are two main types of basic motor vehicle — three and four-wheeled.

Three-wheeled basic motor vehicles

Most three-wheeled basic motor vehicles are based on motor cycle and scooter components. They are made and used in large numbers in Mediterranean countries, such as Italy and Greece, for the haulage of light goods and agricultural produce. They are also made in a number of countries in Asia where they are primarily used as passenger taxis. Engine sizes vary from 50 to 250cc with load capacities up to 500kg. The small wheels and lightweight construction of most of these vehicles limits their use to smooth roads and urban areas. More robust three-wheeled vehicles with large diameter wheels suitable for rural areas are much less common but one example is made in India with a 400cc engine and 750kg load capacity.

Four-wheeled basic motor vehicles

Four-wheeled motor vehicles are made in many developing countries with the assistance of major international vehicle manufacturers. Many are simply assembled from kits of imported components with few locally made items. In a number of countries, however, vehicles with a more basic specification have been introduced which can be made economically in relatively small numbers using a large proportion of locally made parts. These include several which are referred to collectively as BTV's (Basic Transport Vehicles) or AUV's (Asian Utility Vehicles). The lead in their design came from two companies in the United States, Ford and General Motors, and other international manufacturers have now followed. They are designed to be manufactured in developing countries by adding imported drive trains and other critical components to a locally produced chassis and body. As experience is gained, an increasing proportion of the components are made locally.

Engine sizes are generally between 1000 and 1600cc and payloads are 500 to 1000kg. The chassis is easy to fabricate and the body panels are designed to be formed by simple bending processes. A wide variety of bodies can be fitted to the basic chassis and cab for both goods and passenger transport. The manufacture and use of BTV's has been particularly successful in the Philippines, where several different models exist, but they are also produced in other countries in Asia and South America.

Another type of vehicle which can also be considered as a basic motor vehicle is the 'micro' pick-up or van. These were introduced in the mid 1970's by Japanese manufacturers, and they have rapidly become popular in some developing countries because they are significantly cheaper to buy and operate than larger motor vehicles.

As there are such a wide and diverse range of basic motor vehicles in existence, a different format has been adopted for this section. The principal features of the two main types are described above, and a variety of examples with a brief description of each now follows. The advantages and disadvantages of the group as a whole are considered in comparison the other categories of vehicles.

Advantages   -   driver and passengers or load usually protected from weather;
                 -   large load capacity;
                 -   speed up to 90km/hour.
Disadvantages -   relatively complicated and expensive to buy and operate.

Goods vehicle suitable for rural areas. 400cc engine, 750kg load capacity: India.

General purpose light goods vehicle, manufactured in Italy. 500kg load capacity, 220cc engine. The off-road performance of this vehicle is surprisingly good because the engine is positioned between the rear wheels, giving a low centre of gravity and good grip in slippery conditions. Many of the components are similar to those used in scooters.

Urban taxi, known as a 'autorickshaw', manufactured in India. 150-175cc engine, 300-500 kg load capacity, or three passengers. Many components are similar to those used in scooters.

Urban goods vehicle, manufactured in Greece. 50cc engine, 200kg load capacity, also based on scooter components.

Urban taxi with 125cc engine and rust-proof fibreglass body, manufactured in Indonesia.

Urban goods vehicle, used by the Dutch Post Office. Many components are similar to those used in motor cycles.

Light goods/passenger vehicle, manufactured in Vietnam. 600cc engine, 450kg load capacity. Based on components made by Citroen, the French car manufacturer.

Ford AUV, manufactured in the Philippines. This model has a 1300cc engine and 750kg load capacity. Used for carrying goods or passengers.

Japanese 'micro' pick-up, used as an urban 'share' taxi in Indonesia. Engine sizes for this type of vehicle vary from 350- 850cc, with load capacities of 450-700kg.

Agricultural vehicles

POWER SOURCES intended primarily for agricultural activities can often be utilized for transport as well. While such devices may not offer optimum transport performance (because they are not specifically designed for that purpose) they are often attractive to the farmer because they can meet many of his needs without the purchase of a separate vehicle being necessary. This not only saves capital expenditure, but also spreads the fixed cost of owning and operating the equipment over a greater amount of useful work. The dual-purpose nature of agricultural vehicles is all the more useful where the seasonal pattern of agricultural work creates needs for transport and cultivation at different times of the year.

Three types of low-cost agricultural transport are considered here. Wheeled tool carriers are used for cultivation with draught animals, and can be converted into carts by adding load platforms. Single-axle tractors, or power tillers, are used in many countries, most successfully for wet land agriculture, and they can be used for transport by adding trailers. Finally there are examples of semi-permanent vehicles which are powered by engines that have been temporarily removed from single-axle tractors.

Animal drawn tool carrier conversion

Animal drawn tool carrier converted for use as a cart: Sudan.

Animal drawn tool carrier in use for cultivation. Conversion to a cart is time-consuming and may be inconvenient: India.

Description — A flat load platform, and simple container if necessary, is fitted on top of the tool carrier such that it may be attached or removed quickly and easily. The platform should be as low as possible to minimize side loads on the wheels and bearings. As the wheels are normally small (40-60cm in diameter) pneumatic tyres are desirable.

Advantages — simple and cheap.

Disadvantages — load capacity less than purpose-built cart;
— heavier, larger capacity bodies are difficult and time-consuming to fit.

Remarks With an multi-purpose equipment, some compromises in the design have to be accepted due to the conflicting requirements of versatility and optimum performance in each role. In the example shown immediately above, small wheels and low ground clearance are desirable for cultivation, but are a disadvantage when using the equipment as a cart. Also, the load platform is inevitably rather high, which is inconvenient for loading and unloading and increases side loads on the wheels. If cultivation equipment and transport are needed at the same time, or if frequent conversion is necessary, operational compromises are unavoidable.

A separate, purpose-built animal-drawn cart is clearly preferable to a tool carrier conversion – if sufficient finance and animals are available.

Single-axle tractor and trailer

A single axle tractor, normally used for cultivation, pulling a general purpose trailer: Cameroon.

Description: — A wood or steel load container is mounted on two wheels such that the centre of gravity of the load is over the axle. Pneumatic tyres and roller bearings are essential and suspension and brakes are desirable. A hitch is normally provided on the tractor. Most tractors use low-speed, single cylinder diesel engines with power outputs of 6 - 20hp, which are robust and reliable.

Advantages: — high load capacity;
— can be used on rough ground and hills;
— inexpensive and straightforward to maintain.

Disadvantages: — slower and less comfortable than purpose-built vehicles;
— special purpose bodies are difficult and time- consuming to fit;
— difficult to manoeuvre;
— poor braking.

Remarks: Single-axle tractors can carry up to 1500kg at up to 20km/hr and can be used to transport both goods and people. There is normally no protection from the weather for the driver or passengers, but if the tractor is to be used for a long period of time for transport only it may be worthwhile to fit a more elaborate body.

A single-axle tractor and trailer being used to carry a large load of goods and passengers: China.

This single-axle tractor and trailer appears to be a permanent vehicle as so many modifications have been made. Apart from the covered trailer and driver's seat, the exhaust pipe has been extended above the roof and a drive belt guard and wind shield have been fitted, together with a full width seat and luggage box underneath: China.

101

Semi-permanent agricultural vehicle

Three-wheeled semi-permanent vehicle in China. The engine can be removed for other duties.

Description: — The engine on a single-axle tractor is usually easy to remove and replace, and can be incorporated into a purpose-built three or four-wheeled vehicle. The vehicle usually has a steel chassis and a steel or wood body, with an absolute minimum of refinements and which is robust and easy to maintain. High ground clearance is normally provided for use on rough terrain. By incorporating gearing an increase in speed compared with a tractor may be obtained, but there will be a corresponding reduction in load capacity.

Advantages: — easy to manoeuvre and reverse;
— may be faster than tractor and trailer;
— straightforward to maintain.

Disadvantages: — relatively expensive, and can only be used when engine is not required for tractor;
— may have lower load capacity than tractor and trailer.

Remarks: These vehicles have been very widely used in Greece and Crete for transporting farm goods and people in hilly areas. Several thousand three-wheeled vehicles have been built by small-scale manufacturers since the 1960's. Early designs utilized engines from single-axle tractors, but the concept was successful enough to justify built-in engines and more elaborate bodywork in later models. They are capable of carrying about 1000kg at up to 45km/hr. In some countries farmers have made their own vehicles from scrap materials by using a tractor engine.

Three wheeled agricultural vehicle in Germany. As the engine is fitted under the body, it is unlikely to be removed regularly.

This four-wheeled vehicle uses a single-axle tractor engine and was made by a farmer in South Korea. (Photo by S. Kim)

Performance characteristics of low cost vehicles

The following table describes the performance characteristics of the range of low-cost vehicles described in this book.

The figures quoted are a brief summary of what is typical, and they are not claimed to be definitive or comprehensive. With such a wide variety of vehicles, circumstances and geographical locations there will inevitably be considerable local variations.

Vehicle	Relative Cost	Max. load (kg)	Max. speed (km/hr)	Max. range (km)	Route limitations
Shoulder pole	-	35	5	20	Unlimited
Chee-geh	10	50	5	20	Unlimited
Western wheelbarrow	20	100	5	2	Reasonably flat
Chinese wheelbarrow	30	200	5	20	Reasonably flat
Handcart	50-150	200-500	5	20	Reasonably flat, wide track
Standard bicycle	50-90	40	20	60	Reasonably flat
Load-carrying bicycle	60-100	50-200	10-15	30-40	Reasonably flat
Bicycle and trailer	90-150	100	10-15	30-40	Reasonably flat, wide track
Bicycle and sidecar	90-150	150-300	10-15	30-40	Reasonably flat, wide track
Tricycle	150-200	150-300	10-15	30-40	Reasonably flat, wide track
Pack animal	variable	150-400	5	20	Unlimited
Animal sledge	10 (sledge only)	200-400	5	20	Reasonably flat, wide track
Animal cart	100-180 (cart only)	500-3000	5	20	Reasonably flat, wide track
Motorized bicycle	150-200	50-200	20-30	50	Reasonably flat
Motor cycle	250-600	100-150	40-90	100-200	Steep hills
Motor cycle and sidecar/tricycle	350-800	250-500	30-60	80-150	Moderate hills, wide track
Motor cycle and trailer	350-800	250	30-60	80-150	Moderate hills, wide track
Single-axle tractor and trailer	1500	1500	15-20	50	Steep hills, wide track
AUV	4000	500-1000	90	200	Steep hills, wide track

Relative Cost: No currency is quoted or intended. The figures indicate the order of magnitude of cost in relation to other vehicles in the table. For some of the simpler vehicles a significant proportion of the 'cost' to the user may consist of the time needed to make the device, rather than cash outlay.

Maximum Load and Speed: Actual loads and speeds would normally be considerably less than these figures, and the maximum speed is unlikely to be achieved when carrying the maximum load.

Maximum Range: The figure quoted is an assessment of the maximum distance that is likely to be covered in one journey with a typical load, taking into account the physical effort required. Conflicting factors, such as speed, load, physical ability, terrain, route conditions and intensity of need create particularly wide variations in the distances which vehicles are used to cover.

Route Limitations: These descriptions indicate the types of route on which the vehicle can be used.

References

1 King, M., (ed). "Medical care in developing countries. A primer on the medicine of poverty and a symposium from Makerere", (Nairobi, 1966).

2 O'Keefe, M. "Evaluation of medical missions: a pilot project". *Contact,* October 1973.

3 Anon., *Employment, growth and basic needs: a one-world problem.* (International Labour Organization, Geneva, 1976).

4 Anon., "An investigative survey of appropriate rural transport for small farmers in Kenya". (Transportation Department, World Bank, Washington, 1977).

5 Hall, D.D., "Biomass for energy: fuels now and in the future". *Journal of the Royal Society of Arts*, No 5312, CXXX, July 1982, pp. 457-471.

6 National Council of Applied Economic Research., "Transport technology for the rural areas: India." (International Labour Organization, Geneva, July 1981).

7 Cook, C. "Rural mobility and communications in Mexico: interim report." (Transportation and Water Department, World Bank) (mimeo).

8 Anon., "Trends in Road Use in Kenya." (Ministry of Transport and Communications, July 1971, P.47).

9 as ref. 6

9 National Council of Applied Economic Research., "Transport technology for the rural areas: India. (International Labour Organization, Geneva, July 1981).

10 Madhaven, S., "Rural transport in Karnataka with special reference to Kanakapura (Bangalore District), India". *Research Working Paper No. 7,* (School of Social Sciences and Business Studies, Polytechnical of Central London, July 1980).

11 Smith, J.D., *Transport technology and employment in rural Malaysia.* (International Labour Organization, Geneva, December 1981).

12 Adebisi, O., "Transport technology for the rural areas: Nigeria". (International Labour Organization) (mimeo).

13 Anon., "Philippine Islands roads feasibility study, final report (General Text)." (Ministry of Public Highways, March 1980).

14 El-Hawary, M. A., and T.Y. El-reedy, *Rural roads and poverty alleviation in Egypt.* (International Labour Organization, Geneva, 1982).

15 Anon., "Report of the National Transport Planning Committee, Government of India." (May 1980).

16 Anon., "Construction of farm-to-market roads in Pakistan (Umbrella Project)." (Ministry of Local Government and Rural Development, Islamabad, July 1983).

17 Anon., "China non-motorized vehicle." (Bureau of Highways of Ministry of Communications, People's Republic of China, prepared for ESCAP workshop-cum-exhibition on the improvement of non- motorized transport, Bangkok, 8-14 March 1983).

18 Anon., "The use of non-motorized vehicles in Vietnam." (prepared for ESCAP workshop-cum-exhibition on the improvement of non-motorized transport, Bangkok, 8-14 March 1983).